Exploration *and* Encounters

Miss. Grocott

HEINEMANN
EDUCATIONAL

CONTENTS

Heinemann Educational,
a division of Heinemann Educational Books Ltd,
Halley Court, Jordan Hill, Oxford OX2 8EJ

OXFORD LONDON EDINBURGH MADRID
ATHENS BOLOGNA PARIS MELBOURNE
SYDNEY AUCKLAND SINGAPORE TOKYO
IBADAN NAIROBI HARARE GABORONE
PORTSMOUTH NH(USA)

© Rosemary Rees, Sue Styles and Richard
Scollins 1992
The moral right of the proprietors has been
asserted

First published 1992

**British Library Cataloguing in Publication
Data** is available from the British Library on
request.

ISBN 0 435 318012

Designed by Ron Kamen, Green Door Design
Ltd, Basingstoke

Maps by Jeff Edwards, illustration on page 21 by
Dave Barnett

Printed in Spain by Mateu Cromo

Acknowledgements
The author and publisher would like to thank
the following for permission to reproduce
photographs:
Akademische Druk und Verlagsanstalt, Graz:
10A
Ancient Art and Architecture Collection: 4G
(Richard Stirling), 6B, 7G

Arxiu MAS: 8A, 9C, 9E, 11A
Biblioteca Laurenziano, Florence: 6E
Biblioteca Nazionale Centrale, Florence: 5C (M.
Schiopetto)
Bibliothèque Nationale/E. T. Archive: 2A
Bodleian Library, Oxford: 2D, 2E, 4E, 5E, 5F, 7A,
11B, 11C
British Library, London: 1E, 1I, 1J, 2B
Werner Forman Archive: 5D, 5G, 5H, 6A, 7B,
7C, 7E, 7F
Giraudon/Bridgeman Art Library: 4H, 9A
Michael Holford: 3E, 3F, 3G, 6D, 9F
Hubert Josse, Paris: 1G
Ander McIntyre: 4D
Museum für Völkerkunde, Vienna: 7D
Nasa/Science Photo Library: 1A
National Museums and Galleries on
Merseyside: 5B
G. Dagli Orti: 3A, 4A, 4F
Roger-Viollet: 8B, 8C
Royal Geographical Society: 10D
Scala: 9D

Cover illustration: Atlas by Diego Homen,
showing South America and Portugal c. 1558
(British Library/Bridgeman Art Library)

The illustrations on pages 23 (Source C) and 37
are reproduced from *See Through History: The
Aztecs*, Hamlyn Children's Books, 1992.

Every effort has been made to contact copyright
holders of material reproduced in this book.
Any omissions will be rectified in subsequent
printings if notice is given to the publisher.

1 What did people know about the world 500 years ago?

Do you want to be an explorer? Do you want to cut your way through steamy jungles? Do you want to climb the highest mountains in the world? Do you want to tramp across frozen ice-fields? Perhaps you would sooner stay at home. If you want to, you can explore any country in the world. But wherever you go, someone else will have been there before you.

Men and women have made maps of every country and continent. They have measured coasts, rivers and mountains. They have drawn plans of cities, towns and villages. You will have to travel to the planets and the stars if you want to explore unknown places. It was not always like this.

Hundreds of years ago it was difficult to travel anywhere. It was dangerous, too. Merchants and sailors were often away for months and sometimes years. When they got back home they told everyone what they had seen and where they thought they had been. They drew maps and charts. Gradually people living in Europe put together a picture of what they thought the world was like.

Source A

This is a photograph of an astronaut walking on the moon. It was taken in November 1969.

Source B

If there were no obstacles, a man could go round the earth as a fly crawls round an apple.

This was written in the 1200s.

> **Obstacle = Think about an obstacle race. You can't get easily to the end because there are things in the way stopping you from running straight and fast. An obstacle is something which gets in the way.**

PERMIA

MONGUL

FILLANDIA

ROSSIA over SARMATIA

Moschovia

Characoracum

Xandu

NORVEGIA

SVETIA

Riga

CHATAJO

Chambalech

Ixlandia

DATIA

PRUSIA

POLANO

Prago

ROSSIA ROSSA

Deserto Lop

Quian Fl.

Nangin

SCOTIA

OLANDO

UNGARIA

Fl. Danubio

MARE CHASPIUM

Bachu

Fl. Phison over Ganges

HIBERNIA

ANGLIA

Fl. Ren

PONTUS EUSINUS

TEBET

Pareisi

Veniexia

Constantinopoli

GIAVA

OCEANIUS ATHLANTICUS

GALLIA

ITALIA

Roma

ASIA MENOR

ISPANIA

GRETIA

Hierusalem

Fl. Tigris

BANGALA

MARE MEDITERRANEUM

Deserto

BANGALA

Lisbona

Zibiltra

Babilonia

INDIA PRIMA

Fl. Indus

NUMIDIA

LIBIA

EGYPTO

PERSIA

Deli

Canaria

Marrocco

Fl. Nilo

Malabar

Deserto

ARABIA FELIX

TAPRONA over Siometra

MAURITANIA

Aden

Melli

Tambutu

Chalecut

NUBIA

SAYLAM

ABASSIA

MARE

Regno de SABA

INDICUM

Xengibar

DIAB

ETHYOPIA

Source C

Brother Mauro, an Italian monk, drew this map of the world in 1459.

Many people thought that the world was flat and round – like a saucer. They said that if you travelled too far, you would fall over the edge and never be seen again. Other people, and most sailors, had worked out that the world was round – like a ball.

Activities

1 Look at Brother Mauro's map. Work out the modern names of the countries, cities and seas on his map.

2 Which parts of Brother Mauro's map look like a present-day map of the world?

3 Which parts of Brother Mauro's map are NOT like the present-day map?

4 Why do you think Brother Mauro's map is different from the present-day map?

5 Why did some people in the 1400s believe that the world was flat like a saucer?

Merchants, sailors and travellers told tales about the wonderful things they had seen and the strange people they had met.

Source
D
We saw on the shore a huge giant who danced, leaped and sang, while throwing sand and dust over his head. He had a large face, painted round with red; his eyes were ringed with yellow and in the middle of his cheeks were painted two hearts. He had hardly any hair on his head, what little he had being painted white.

Antonio Pigafetta wrote this. He went round the world with the explorer Magellan between 1519 and 1522.

Source
F
There is another isle where people have one foot, and that foot is so broad it covers all the body and shades it from the Sun. On this foot they run so fast it is a wonder to see.

From a book written by Sir John Mandeville in about 1360. He said he had travelled around the world for 35 years, but a lot of his book was copied from earlier books.

Source
E

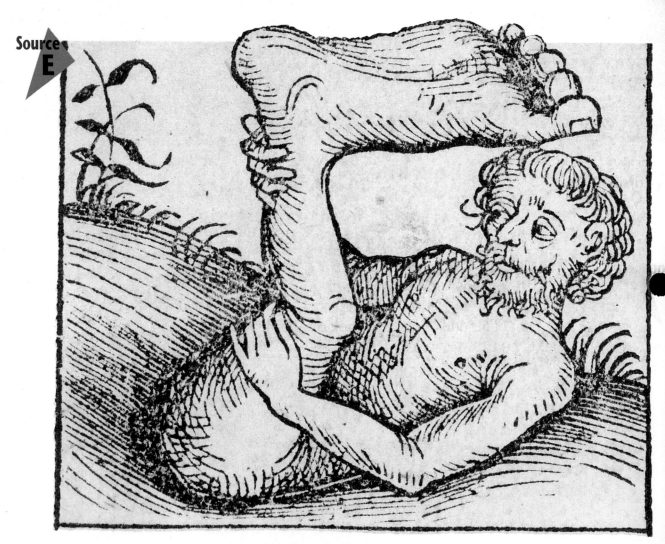

This was drawn by Hartman Schedel in 1493.

Source G

This painting shows Europeans arriving in far distant lands. It was painted in about 1400.

Source H

In the harbour there are some very white and beautiful people, who wear boots and hats of iron and never stay in any place. They eat a sort of white stone and drink blood.

A man living in Sri Lanka wrote this in the 16th century about some visitors to his country.

Activities

1   Most people like stories. When people tell stories, they are not always true. Do you think Antonio Pigafetta (Source D) **really** saw the giant? Read the description of the giant carefully. Draw a picture of him.

2   Look at Source E and read Source F. Do you think that Sebastian Munster and Sir John Mandeville both saw these people with odd feet?

3   Now look at Source G. Do you think the people in the middle of the picture really looked like this once upon a time? If they didn't, why were they put in the picture?

4   Read Source H. Who do you think the man from Sri Lanka was describing?

Olaus Magnus drew this map in 1572.

Activity

Why were most people in the 1500s frightened of travelling to unknown lands? Was it only because of monsters?

A lot of people were frightened by the stories told by merchants and sailors. Many men and women believed that if you sailed north you would go into a world of darkness. The seas would turn solid and your blood would freeze. If you travelled south the seas would boil and your skin would be burned black. If you travelled east, overland into Asia, you might be attacked by natives or eaten by wild animals. If you travelled west, into the great **Ocean Sea** (the Atlantic Ocean), you would make the most frightening journey it was possible to make. You would sail into seas full of huge monsters, and would probably never be seen again.

People were frightened about things they did not know or understand. They were frightened, too, of things which they knew really happened. People knew that terrible storms wrecked ships and drowned sailors. They knew that sailors caught all kinds of diseases and often died on long voyages. Only very brave people dared to travel into the unknown.

Source I

Some people believed that sea monsters wrecked ships and drowned sailors.

How do we know?

You have seen strange maps and even stranger drawings of monsters and odd-looking people. You have read what men said about people in unknown lands.

1 Copy this table into your book. Match up the sentences with the sources which tell you the same thing.

Write in the right-hand column the name of the source which tells you about these ideas.

Sentence	Source
People knew more about Europe than about Africa and India.	
People thought that there were strange-looking people in far distant lands.	
People believed in sea monsters which attacked ships.	

2 Why do you think people drew monsters on their maps?

2 Why did Columbus sail west? What did he find there?

When you next go to your local shop or supermarket look for the shelf where the spices are kept. Five or six hundred years ago these spices cost a lot of money. So did goods like silk and silver, diamonds and ivory. Only rich people could afford to buy them.

Merchants and traders brought goods into Europe from China, India and the Spice Islands. Europeans called this part of the world 'the Indies'. Some merchants travelled overland between Europe and the Indies. They travelled across hot deserts and over rocky mountains. Some sent their goods by ships. All journeys were difficult and sometimes dangerous. They took a very long time.

Source A

A picture painted during the 1400s. It shows people gathering peppers to sell to a European merchant.

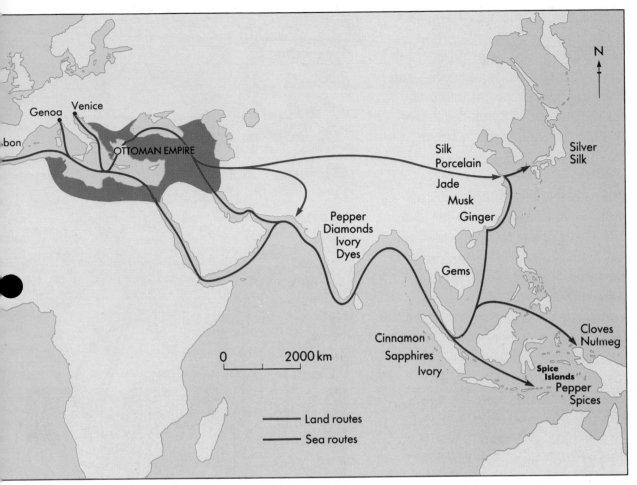

Genoa Venice

..bon

OTTOMAN EMPIRE

Pepper
Diamonds
Ivory
Dyes

Silk
Porcelain

Jade
Musk
Ginger

Silver
Silk

Gems

Cinnamon
Sapphires
Ivory

Cloves
Nutmeg

**Spice
Islands**
Pepper
Spices

N

0   2000 km

——— Land routes
——— Sea routes

This modern map shows what merchants and traders bought in the Indies, and the routes they took to get there and back again to Europe.

All the trade routes to Europe from the Indies went through lands called the **Ottoman Empire**. The rulers of the Ottoman Empire made the traders and merchants pay large taxes on the goods they were carrying. The merchants had to charge extra high prices for their goods when they got back to Europe. Soon even very rich people would not be able to buy goods from the Indies. Someone had to find a new route to the East.

Activities

1 Look at Source A. Which is the merchant? How do you know?

2 Look at the map.
   a Make lists of all the things which the merchants brought back to Europe under these headings:
      Spices   Jewels   Others.
   b Why do you think these things were so expensive in the 1400s?

3 The journeys which the traders made in the 1400s were long and dangerous. Why do you think they took such risks?

Christopher Columbus grew up in the busy port of Genoa, Italy. He learned to sail ships, to steer by the stars and to work out speed and distance at sea. Columbus worked out that he could reach the Indies by sailing west across the great Ocean Sea.

Queen Isabella of Spain said she would give Columbus money to do this. He used her money to hire three ships, called the *Pinta*, the *Nina* and the *Santa Maria*. He also hired 90 men and boys to sail them. In August 1492 they all set out from Spain, into the unknown.

Two months later, after sailing westwards all the time, the ship's look-out saw land. Columbus was sure he had got to the Indies. He rowed ashore with the other captains. When they landed they all thanked God, kissed the sand, and set up the royal banner of Spain.

The people who lived there told Columbus he had landed on an island called **Guanahani**. They were Arawak people. Columbus called them 'Indians' because he was sure he had found the Indies. He called the island San Salvador.

In January 1493 Columbus sailed back to Europe. He took with him gold and jewels, birds, plants and even some Indians. They came from the islands he had explored.

Source B

This woodcut shows Columbus sailing by some of the islands near San Salvador.

Source C

Half an hour before sunrise, I set my course for the Canary Islands, which are in the Ocean Sea, from there to set off on a voyage that will last until I arrive in the Indies.

Columbus kept a journal. In it he wrote down what happened each day. This is part of what he wrote on 3 August 1492.

This picture shows Columbus landing on the island he called San Salvador. It was drawn in 1594.

Most people thought Columbus had found a way to the Indies by sailing west. Some people were puzzled. They thought that Columbus had not sailed far enough to have reached the Indies. He hadn't brought any silks or spices back with him, either. Just where had he been?

Activities

1 Look at your classroom globe or a big map of the world. Can you find the Indies? Which way would Columbus have to sail to get from Spain to the Indies?

2 Look at Source D. Here are some words which you could use to describe Columbus in the picture:
   Powerful   Proud   Important

   a Think of three good words to describe the Indians in the drawing.
   b Do you think it was really like this when Columbus landed?

3 Two of the Indians in the drawing are talking to each other. What do you think they are saying?

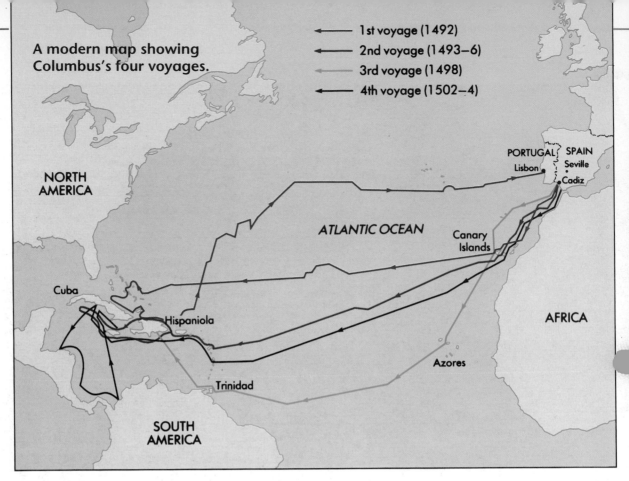

A modern map showing Columbus's four voyages.

1st voyage (1492)
2nd voyage (1493–6)
3rd voyage (1498)
4th voyage (1502–4)

NORTH AMERICA

ATLANTIC OCEAN

PORTUGAL   SPAIN
Lisbon   Seville
            Cadiz

Canary Islands

Cuba

Hispaniola

AFRICA

Azores

Trinidad

SOUTH AMERICA

Christopher Columbus crossed the Ocean Sea three more times. On the map you can see the different routes he sailed and the places he explored. Each voyage made Columbus more sure than ever that he had reached the Indies. He thought that islands like Cuba, Hispaniola and Trinidad were just off the coast of China. He was wrong.

Columbus's fourth voyage ended in 1504. He never went to sea again. Queen Isabella was dying. Her husband, King Ferdinand, was not interested in Columbus. He knew that Columbus had not found a way to the Indies by sailing west across the Ocean Sea. He thought that Columbus had failed. Columbus died two years later. He never knew that he had been exploring a whole world which hardly anyone in Europe had guessed was there.

Soon, men like Robert Thorne were drawing maps which were very different from the one drawn by Brother Mauro in 1459 (see page 5).

This map was drawn by an Englishman,
Robert Thorne, in 1527.

What do people say about the past?

When people write about the past they do not always agree. Read what these people are saying.

1 Can you find any differences in what Hank and Ilsa are saying?

2 Hank says that Columbus was the first person to discover America. Do you agree ?

3 Copy this table into your book. Which of these sentences are *fact* and which are a *point of view*? Write **fact, point of view or don't know** in the right-hand column by each sentence.

'In 1492 Christopher Columbus sailed over the Atlantic Ocean. He was the first person to discover America. He was one of the greatest explorers who ever lived.'

Hank

Ilsa

'In 1000 AD the Vikings landed in North America.'

Sentences	
In 1492 Christopher Columbus sailed over the Atlantic Ocean.	
Columbus was one of the greatest explorers who ever lived.	
In 1000 AD the Vikings landed in North America.	

3 What was life like on board ship 500 years ago?

This painting of caravels was made in the 1500s.

Caravels were the best ships for making ocean voyages. They were small, fast and easy to steer. Two of Christopher Columbus's first ships, the *Pinta* and the *Nina*, were caravels. Life for the sailors on a caravel was tough. It was also dangerous. There were violent storms. Ships were often wrecked. Every day began with prayers. The sailors prayed that they would be kept safe from harm.

Caravels were about 21 metres long and 6.5 metres wide. Below decks the crew had to store all the food and drink they would need on the voyage. They also had to store the sails, ropes and firewood. There had to be room for the **tiller** and the **anchor**. There had to be room, too, for any treasure they might bring back.

Sailors lived and slept on the open deck, no matter what the weather was like. They usually had one hot meal a day, which was cooked on deck. They ate the fresh food at the start of the voyage, before it went bad. Then they ate hard ship's biscuit, salted meat and fish. Rats and maggots usually got to the food, while it was stored in the hold. The sailors drank water or water mixed with wine. The water was stored in wooden barrels. After a week or two it tasted bad. The wine sometimes turned into vinegar.

Sailors got terrible diseases and many of them died. In hot parts of the world they were sometimes ill with **malaria** and **yellow fever**. The disease they got most often was **scurvy**. This was because they could not eat fresh fruit or vegetables on long voyages. No one knew, then, why sailors got scurvy. They only knew that it was a dreadful illness.

We ate only old biscuit reduced to powder, all full of worms and stinking of the urine that the rats made on it. And we drank water that was yellow and stinking.

Antonio Pigafetta wrote this in the 1500s. He sailed across the Pacific Ocean with Magellan. He is telling what they ate when they had been at sea for nearly four months.

It rotted all my gums, which gave out a black and putrid blood. My thighs and lower legs were black, and I was forced to use my knife each day to cut into the flesh, to release this black and foul blood.

A 15th-century sailor describes what it was like to have scurvy.

Activities

1 Life wasn't easy for sailors 500 years ago. Make a list of all the problems they faced on a voyage.

2 Sailors in the 1500s often became very ill. Read this page again. Explain why so many sailors became ill and died.

This is a modern photograph of a sand-glass which is about 500 years old.

The crew of about 30 sailors was divided into two groups. Each group was called a **watch**. A watch worked for four hours and then rested for four hours. While one watch rested, the other watch worked. Time was measured by a **half-hour sand glass**. It was the job of the ship's boy to turn the glass over as the sand ran out. He had to shout out the time, too.

All wooden ships leak. The first job of each watch was to pump the sea water out. If there were any gaps between the wooden planks, the crew filled them with rope and sealed them with hot tar. They scrubbed the decks and pulled on heavy ropes to move the sails. Sometimes, when the weather was very bad, they had to pull the sails down; when the weather was better and the wind blowing in the right direction, they put the sails up again. The watch checked the cargo. They mended sails and ropes. Some sailors were look-outs. They climbed to the **crow's nest** at the top of the mast. Their job was to shout out if they saw land, or another ship, or any kind of danger.

Activity

Look very carefully at the picture opposite.

Write a few sentences describing what is happening on board the ship.

◄ **Life on board ship was hard and dangerous 500 years ago.**

In the 1500s it was very difficult to take a ship from place to place if the captain could not see land. Sailors made charts of the sea routes to all the places they most often visited. But ships sailing into unknown seas had no charts to help them. How did they manage?

All ships had a **compass**. This told the captain whether his **helmsman** was steering north, south, east or west. Many sailors used a **quadrant**. This told the sailors how far north of the equator they were.

Source **G**

This is a photograph of a compass used in the 1500s.

Source **F**

This is a photograph of a traverse board used in the 1500s. Details about the direction a ship was sailing, and the distance it had travelled, were pegged out on a traverse board. The traverse board was always propped up in front of the helmsman.

Sailors needed to work out how fast their ship was travelling. They dropped a piece of wood over the side. They used a sand-glass to measure the time it took for the ship to pass the wood. On some ships a long piece of rope was tied to a log of wood. **Knots** were tied in the rope. A sailor threw the wood over the side. He timed the speed at which the knots ran through his hands. This way he knew how fast the ship was sailing and could work out how far it had sailed.

This modern drawing shows the helmsman's table. Can you see the compass, sand-glass, and traverse board? The helmsman used all these to steer the ship. He obeyed his captain's orders. The captain checked the compass and traverse board. He checked the readings made from the quadrant. Then he decided what course the helmsman had to steer. He kept a careful note of everything in his **log book**. He would be blamed if anything went wrong.

Activity

Navigation was a very skilled job. Describe what sailors did with each of these instruments: compass, quadrant, sand-glass, traverse board.

Which of these would be the most difficult to use?

Were things different then?

1 Make a big picture which shows:
  a a modern passenger ship
  b a ship used by people to cross the seas before the time of Columbus
  c a caravel.

2 Find as many differences as you can between the modern ship and the caravel.

3 What differences can you find between a caravel and one of the ships used before the time of Columbus?

4 Life on board ship was different in fine weather and in a storm. Make a drawing or write a paragraph to show some of these differences.

4 Who were the Aztecs?

The islands Christopher Columbus explored were not empty lands. People lived there. It was the same on the mainland of America. Look back to the map on page 14. Can you find Columbus's 4th voyage? He sailed along the coast of Central America. There were many different groups of people living there. Some were hunters and some were farmers. Some lived in towns, and some wandered from place to place. The **Aztecs** were one of the strongest and most powerful groups. Columbus did not know this. Neither did the Europeans who followed him to America.

The Aztec people had not always been strong and powerful. For hundreds of years they had wandered from place to place. They were looking for somewhere to settle. In about the year 1300 they came to the Valley of **Mexico** and **Lake Texcoco**. They moved on to swampy islands in the middle of the lake. The Aztecs fished and farmed. They built houses from sticks and reeds covered with mud. They built a temple for one of their gods, **Source A Huitzilopochtli.** They were on Lake Texcoco to stay; they were not going to move on.

This Aztec picture shows Aztec chiefs setting out on their journey to find a new land.

The Aztec god, Huitzilopochtli, told the Aztec chiefs that they had to travel south. There they would build a large city on a swamp. Huitzilopochtli said that the Aztecs would know when they had come to the right place. This was because they would see an eagle sitting on a cactus. The eagle would be eating a snake. As soon as the Aztecs saw the eagle, the cactus and the snake, they were to stop their wanderings and build a city. The Aztecs wandered until they came to Lake Texcoco. There they were chased onto an island by an angry ruler. On the island they saw, in a cave, the eagle, the cactus and the snake. They knew they had to build a city and settle down.

This is the Aztecs' story about the way they came to live on an island in the middle of Lake Texcoco.

This is a modern drawing of the Aztec god Huitzilopochtli.

Activities

1 Source D is a picture of the badge used by Mexico today. The modern country of Mexico covers the lands where the Aztecs lived. Describe this badge.

2 Read Source B and look again at Source D. Why do you think that Mexico uses this badge today?

This is the modern badge of Mexico.

The Aztecs fought and fought until they captured all the lands, towns and villages for hundreds of miles around Lake Texcoco. The Aztecs forced the rulers of the towns they had defeated to send **tribute** to them. They drew up detailed lists showing exactly what goods each town had to pay to the Aztec state. These goods might be animal skins, black beans, blankets, red peppers, jade beads or shields. The defeated people became poor. They hated the Aztecs. They were also terrified of them. The Aztecs become very rich and very powerful. They called their lands **nahuac**.

The Aztecs built a beautiful city on their island in the middle of Lake Texcoco. They turned the whole island into a city, which they called **Tenochtitlan**. They used mud to make the island bigger and they dug canals to connect up different parts of their island city. They built an enormous **aqueduct** to bring fresh water to the city. They built huge **causeways** to join Tenochtitlan to the mainland.

The Aztecs built big stone temples and beautiful palaces, houses for ordinary people, a zoo and gardens full of brightly-coloured flowers. By 1502 about 300,000 people lived and worked in Tenochtitlan. It was bigger than any city in Europe at that time.

This is an Aztec tribute sheet. It shows what some towns had to pay the Aztecs. The towns are drawn in the left-hand column. By the side of each town are pictures of the things which the Aztecs wanted.

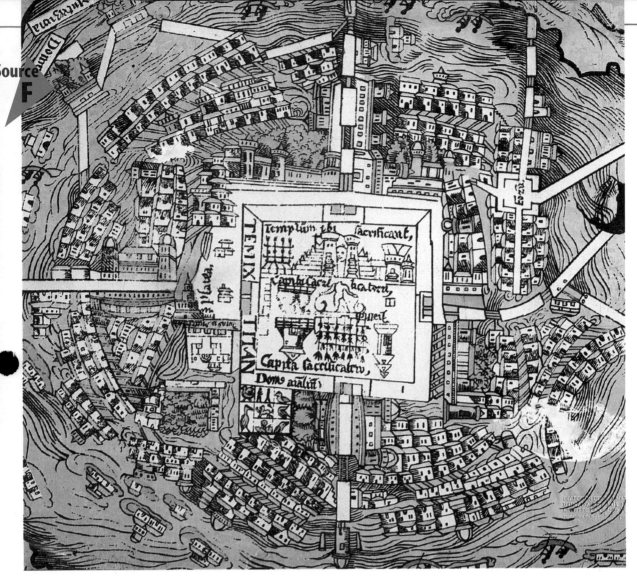

This plan of Tenochtitlan was printed in Germany in 1523.
It was copied from a sketch made by a European, Hernan
Cortes, who visited Tenochtitlan a few years earlier.

Activities

1 a Look at Source E. Can you work
out what the pictures show?

 b Today people pay money to the
government. We call this a 'tax'.
Why do we pay our taxes in
money rather than goods?

 c What sort of things do you think
people today would use, instead
of money, to pay tax? Draw a
picture, like the Aztec tribute
sheet, to show these.

2 Look at the map of Tenochtitlan
(Source F). Can you find the
aqueduct? How many causeways
can you find? What different sorts
of buildings are there?

3 Try to think of all the **good** things
about living on an island like this.
Then think of all the **bad** things.
Write them down in two lists.

The Aztec emperor was chosen by the noble families. The person they chose had to be a nobleman. He had to be a trained priest and a good fighter. In 1502 the noble families chose **Montezuma** to be their emperor.

The Aztecs treated Montezuma as if he was a god. He wore the finest clothes. His sandals had soles made from pure gold. When he travelled outside his palace he was carried on a richly decorated throne by four nobles. No one was allowed to look directly at his face.

Montezuma had a huge palace. Hundreds of people lived and worked there. At mealtimes his servants had to cook more than 1,000 plates of food. Montezuma ate the very best food. Sometimes his advisors stood by his table and talked to him while he ate. They were not allowed to look at him. If he offered them food, they had to eat it standing up. Montezuma drank chocolate after a meal. No one in Europe had ever seen chocolate.

While Montezuma was emperor, the Aztec empire grew bigger than ever before. Montezuma was very rich and very powerful.

This is a modern photograph of the great feather headdress which Montezuma wore in processions.

This picture, made in 1502, shows Montezuma being crowned emperor.

How did things change?

1 These sentences are all about the story of the Aztecs which you have read about in this unit. Put them in the order in which the events happened.

- *The Aztecs built Tenochtitlan in the middle of Lake Texcoco.*
- *The Aztecs chose Montezuma to be their emperor.*
- *Aztec chiefs set out on a journey to find a new land.*
- *The Aztecs forced the rulers they had defeated to send tribute to them.*

2 Make a timeline like this in your book.

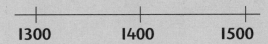

| 1300 | 1400 | 1500 |

Decide where each of the events in Question 1 belongs on your timeline. Draw a picture of the event in the right place.

3 The Aztecs' way of life changed a lot between 1300 and 1500. Some things stayed the same.
Read the sentences in the left-hand column. Copy them into your book. These sentences are about the Aztecs' way of life. If you think this changed between 1300 and 1500 put **changed** in the right-hand column. If you think it didn't change put **stayed the same** in the right-hand column.

Sentences	
Where the Aztecs lived *How strong and powerful they were* *The language they spoke* *The gods they believed in* *The food they ate*	

5 What was life like in the Aztec Empire?

A modern painting of the market in Tenochtitlan.

Every day a great market was held in the centre of Tenochtitlan. Merchants and traders, farmers and craftworkers brought goods to the market from all over the Aztec empire. They brought luxuries like jade necklaces, silver bracelets and golden drinking beakers. They brought ordinary things like black beans, flour, rabbits, puppies, pottery dishes and tobacco pipes. They brought slaves and put them in cages for people to look at and buy. Every day more than 60,000 people went to the market.

The Aztecs did not use money. They took their goods to market to swap them for what they wanted. If two Aztecs couldn't make an exact swap, one of them would add in a few cocoa beans. As a rough guide to the number of beans needed, Aztecs agreed that 100 cocoa beans were worth 1 cloak; a slave was worth 25 cloaks, and a jade necklace was worth 600 cloaks.

Look at the people in the picture opposite. The Aztecs had very strict rules about clothes. Nobles were allowed to wear brightly-coloured cloaks and richly patterned loin-cloths. Ordinary people had to make their clothes from plain, undyed cloth. The Aztecs had strict rules about hairstyles, too. Girls could have their hair loose; as soon as a girl married she had to plait her hair and wind the plaits around her head. Warriors tied their hair in a topknot. They were allowed to wear jewels in their lips, ears and noses at special times.

This is an Aztec picture of a merchant. Some merchants worked for the government. They brought back information about plots and rebellions in far-away towns. They brought back information about strangers who had arrived in the Aztec empire.

Activity

Look at Source A. Choose a scene in the picture. What are the people in your scene doing? Write some sentences to describe what they are doing.

Poor Aztecs lived in one roomed houses on the edge of Tenochtitlan. The walls of their houses were made from **wattle and daub**. Richer people, like craftworkers, lived closer to the middle of Tenochtitlan. Their houses were built with mud-bricks and had rooms which led on to a central courtyard. Nobles lived in palaces in the middle of Tenochtitlan which were built from stone. Most of the palaces had over 100 rooms and courtyards and patios which were full of flowers. The stone walls were decorated with carvings.

Source C

This is an Aztec picture of a bath-house. Most rich Aztecs built one in their garden. They lit fires around the outside until the walls were red hot. Then they went inside and splashed water on the walls to make steam. In the steam they beat themselves with twigs until their skin was clean.

Source D

This is a carved statue of the god Xiuhtectuhtli. Aztecs used to put statues like this by the fireplace in their homes. They called them household gods.

Aztecs did not have much furniture. Everyone slept on mats on the floor. They sat on cushions filled with straw. The most important part of all Aztec houses was the fireplace. This was where the cooking was done. Aztecs ate **tortillas**, which were a sort of pancake made from maize flour. They ate a lot of vegetables, fish and frogs, tadpoles and newts. On special occasions they might roast a duck, a rabbit, a chicken or a puppy. Rich people often ate pheasant and wild pig. Everyone ate with their fingers.

Aztec parents were very strict with their children. They taught them at home. The children learned the sorts of things they would need to do when they were grown-up. Boys were taught fishing and woodwork; girls were taught cooking and weaving. Every boy had to go to school when he was eight. Some boys went to schools where they learned how to be priests. Other boys went to schools where they learned how to be warriors. Girls did not have to go to school. Girls could learn to be priestesses and healers if they went to school.

Source
E

This Aztec picture shows fathers teaching their sons, and mothers teaching their daughters.

Source
F

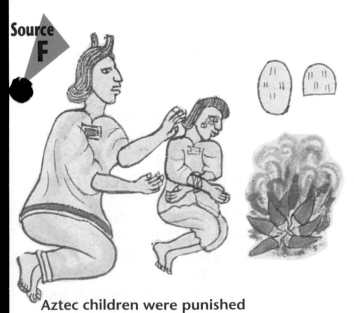

Aztec children were punished by their parents when they were naughty. Sometimes they were pricked with thorns.

Activity

Look at Source E.

a What are the fathers teaching the boys to do?
b What are the mothers teaching the girls to do?
c Are you taught to do these things?

Aztecs did not use letters to make words when they wrote. Instead they drew tiny pictures called **glyphs** to show what they wanted to say. There were very strict rules which all writers had to follow. Each picture was always drawn in the same way, so everyone knew what the writer meant.

Aztecs who were very good at reading and writing could become **scribes**. They could then do important work for the government. They could write down the empire's laws or write out the tribute sheets. All priests could read and write well. They had to write religious books and history books. Aztec books are called **codices**. They were made out of bark paper or deer-skin. The pages were joined together in a long zig-zag.

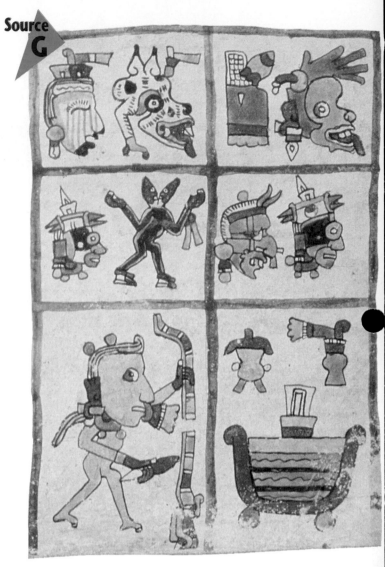

Source G

These are some of the glyphs used by the Aztecs.

Source H

The Aztecs stuck pieces of paper together to make a long book called a codex.

Aztec nobles played a game called **tlachtli** at special times like religious festivals. Two teams played on a stone court surrounded by stone walls. To score, one team had to get a small bouncing rubber ball into the other team's end of the court. The game would be won at once if one side managed to get the ball through their opponent's stone ring, which was fixed high on a wall. The players were only allowed to touch the ball with their knees, elbows or hips. The game was fierce and fast. Players were often hurt and sometimes killed. Everyone came to watch and cheer on their team.

All Aztecs played a game called **patolli**. They had to throw dice and move coloured beans on a board until they got three beans in a row. Many Aztecs lost all they had playing patolli. They and their families had to become slaves.

Were things different then?

1 Choose one of the following:
   - *Aztec children*
   - *Aztec food*
   - *Aztec games*
   - *Aztec houses for rich and poor*

Make a big picture about the part of the Aztec way of life you have chosen. Make sure that you label your picture so that other people will know what it is. Use glyphs for this if you can.

2 Poor Aztecs' lives were quite different from rich Aztecs' lives. Aztec nobles lived differently from the rich Aztecs. See if you can find things in the lives of **all** these Aztecs which were similar. Write a paragraph to say what these are.

Source 1

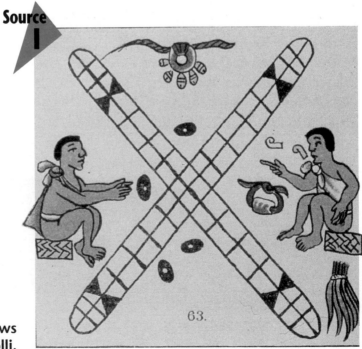

This Aztec picture shows people playing patolli.

6 What did the Aztecs believe?

Source A

The Aztecs believed in many gods and goddesses. Each one looked after a different part of Aztec life. Three gods were more important than all the others. **Huitzilopochtli** was the god of sun and war. **Tezcatlipoca** was the god of night and evil. **Quetzalcoatl** was the god of life. Aztecs believed that one day Quetzalcoatl would come to earth to decide what was to happen to all the Aztec people.

This is a photograph of a modern copy of an Aztec temple.

The Aztecs believed their gods watched them all the time. They were afraid of doing something to make their gods angry. They built huge stone **pyramids**. At the top of each one they built a **temple** for religious **ceremonies** and **sacrifices**. Aztecs believed their gods wanted human blood. Aztec priests sacrificed thousands of men, women and children in the temples. In wars the Aztecs captured people for sacrifice. Aztecs thought that if they did not give human hearts and blood to the gods, then the gods would destroy the world.

Source B

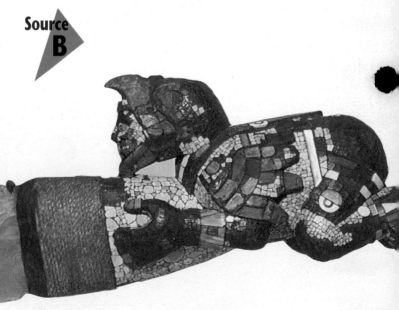

This Aztec knife was used in temple sacrifices.

R S COLLINS

A modern painting of an Aztec sacrifice.

Priests were very powerful people. The emperor did not go to war until he had asked their advice. People asked a priest before they went on a journey or named a baby. Aztecs believed that some days were lucky and some unlucky. It would be terrible to do something important on an unlucky day.

Only the priests could tell them which days were lucky and unlucky. This was because only the priests understood the **sacred calendar**. A baby born on day *4 Dog*, for example, would do well; one born on *2 Rabbit* would become a drunk. A good day for painters was *7 Flower*, and merchants always had to travel on *1 Ocelot*. Priests used the sacred calendar to tell the future too – whether there was going to be a flood, or an earthquake or an invasion. Priestesses worked with the priests. They could do everything the priests did, except make sacrifices.

As well as the sacred calendar, the Aztecs had a sun calendar which they called **haab**. This divided the year into 365 days. Every 52 years the first day of the sacred calendar and the first day of the sun calendar were on the same day. The Aztecs were afraid that on this day the world would end.

Source D

An Aztec statue of Coatlicue, their Earth goddess.

Source E

An Aztec picture showing a man in year 52. He is getting ready for the end of the world by throwing away all his goods.

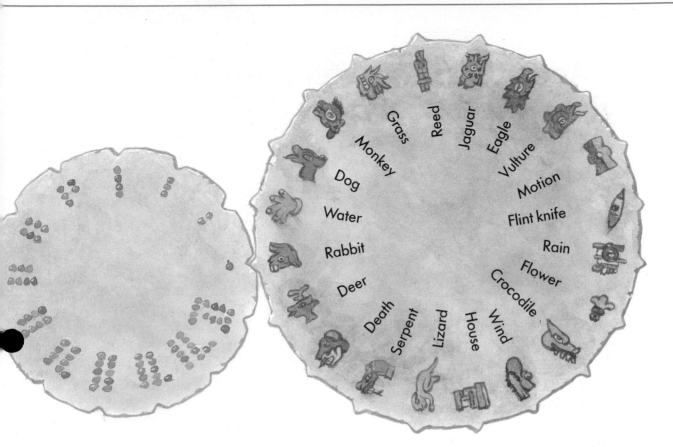

The calendar wheel (large wheel, clockwise from top): Reed, Jaguar, Eagle, Vulture, Motion, Flint knife, Rain, Flower, Crocodile, Wind, House, Lizard, Serpent, Death, Deer, Rabbit, Water, Dog, Monkey, Grass

This shows you how the sacred calendar works. The calendar is made up of two wheels. The small wheel on the left has thirteen numbers painted on it. The large wheel on the right has the names of twenty days painted on it. The small wheel turns clockwise. The large wheel turns anti-clockwise. Each number then fits with a day.

Why did things happen?

1 Aztec priests were very powerful. Read this unit again. Find as many reasons as you can why the priests were so important. Make a list of your reasons under these headings:

War   Travelling   Things in the future

2 What did the Aztecs think would happen if they did not take notice of what their priests said?

7 Aztec craft and technology: what did they make?

This Aztec picture shows fathers teaching their sons special craft skills.

Aztecs did not use money. People were thought to be rich if they owned beautiful things. So an Aztec who owned two bowls with gold and black decorations painted on them was richer than one who had ten ordinary pottery bowls. Rich Aztecs employed the very best **craftworkers** to make the things they needed. Craftworkers were very important people in the Aztec empire.

Different groups of people living in the Aztec empire were better at some crafts than others. The **Mixtecs**, for example, were skilled goldworkers. The people of **Cholula** made the very best pottery. All craftworkers were respected by the other Aztecs. Craftworkers lived and worked in their own separate areas of Aztec cities. They worshipped their own gods. Usually whole families worked at the same craft. Parents taught their children the special skills they needed.

The Aztecs built palaces and temples from stone. Look back at page 34 and you will see one of the temples. Aztec stoneworkers made beautiful and complicated carvings too. They made carvings of their gods (look at page 36). They made carvings of dragons, strange beasts and patterns to decorate their temples and palaces. They made carvings about their history and the way they thought the Aztec world would end.

The Aztecs did not have wheels, so they could not use carts or pulleys to carry and lift the stone they used in building. Slaves carried everything. Aztecs did not have iron from which to make knives and chisels to cut and carve their stone. They used blades made from a mixture of copper and tin or from polished **obsidian**.

Source B

The great Calendar Stone, which told how the Aztec world would end. It was once painted in bright colours.

Activities

1 a Find pictures of beautiful things which rich Aztecs would want to have in their homes. Make a list of these things. Would you want to have them in your home?

 b What do you think the rich Aztecs would give to the craftworkers in return for these things?

2 Copy out this paragraph and fill in the blanks. Use all of the words in the box below to do this.

The Aztecs did not have _____. So they made their knife-blades from _____ and _____. They did not have _____ to carry things. _____ carried everything for them.

slaves obsidian tin carts copper iron

Source C

A carving on the temple of Quetzalcoatl at Teotihuacan.

Aztecs were experts at working with feathers. They used feathers to make huge shields and headdresses which were worn by Aztec kings, nobles and warriors at special times. Look back at page 26 and you will see the headdress which Montezuma wore. Aztecs also used feathers to decorate the clothes of rich people. Sometimes the featherworkers used so many feathers that a whole cloak or skirt looked as if it was made out of feathers and nothing else. Featherworkers made complete outfits for warriors to wear in battle. Some workers made pictures out of feathers. The very best feathers to use were the ones from the green **quetzal** bird and those from the blue **hummingbird**.

Source D

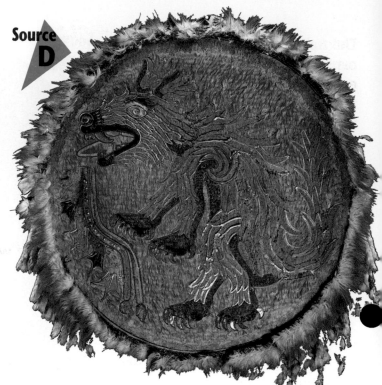

This feather shield belonged to an Aztec king.

Source E

Aztec potters made beautifully shaped bowls, dishes, jugs and drinking cups. They usually painted richly coloured patterns and pictures on the outsides of the pots.

Aztecs did not use wheels at all. They did not use potters' wheels. They made coil pots. When a pot was the right shape, the potter smoothed the outside until there were no bumps left.

Goldsmiths made delicate gold ornaments. They made gold earrings, necklaces, **nose plugs** and **lip plugs** for nobles and important warriors. They made all kinds of wonderful objects for priests, kings and emperors.

Aztecs worked with precious stones like **rubies**. They used **jade** and **turquoise** to make beautiful masks, ornaments and jewellery.

Source F

This snake was made from wood and then covered in turquoise. It was part of an Aztec headdress.

Source G

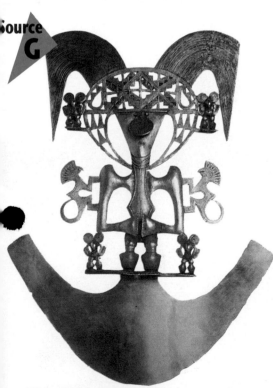

This gold ornament was made by the Mixtec people.

How do we know?

1 Look at Source A on page 38. This shows fathers teaching their sons craft skills. The crafts shown are woodcarving, painting, goldworking and jewellery-making. Work out which picture shows which craft.

2 All the sources in this unit show Aztec craftwork. Put the heads and tails of these sentences together.

Heads	Tails
Source C shows	that the Aztecs were skilled woodcarvers.
Source D shows	that the Aztecs were good at stone carving.
Source E shows	that the Aztecs were skilled goldworkers.
Source F shows	Aztecs were experts at working with feathers.
Source G shows	that the Aztecs were skilled at making pots.

3 Choose **one** source in this unit which you think is most useful for showing us how skilful the Aztec craftworkers were. Say why you think this source is more useful than the others.

8 How did Cortes and his men conquer the Aztec Empire?

Hernan Cortes was ten years old when news reached his town in Spain that Christopher Columbus had crossed the great Ocean Sea. As Cortes grew up he heard stories of a great empire in the West, full of gold and jewels. He longed to go there. He went first to Cuba. There he worked hard and became rich and important. He owned farms and mines. He wanted more than anything to rule a land of his own. Then the governor of Cuba asked him to lead an expedition to the mainland. This was Cortes's great chance.

In 1519 Cortes sailed for Mexico. He took with him 11 ships and 100 sailors, 508 soldiers, 16 horses, a few cannons and some muskets. They all landed safely on a part of Mexico which had not been explored before. Cortes burnt all the ships which had brought them there. There was no going back.

Source A

A painting of Cortes and his men in Mexico. It was painted in 1698.

guʒmã.   mıcɦʋ acã.

This Aztec picture shows Cortes fighting.

Then Cortes ordered some of his men to stay behind. Cortes and 400 Spaniards began their long march to Tenochtitlan. They marched through steamy hot jungles. They marched over high mountains where the winds were icy. They fought off attacks by thousands of fierce Indian warriors. Cortes and his men always won. They used **muskets**, which the Indians had never seen before. They rode horses, which the Indians had never seen before. The Indians were amazed. They began to believe that Cortes was a god. Different Indian tribes agreed to fight with Cortes against the Aztecs, whom they hated and feared. (Look back at page 24 to remind yourself why.) Meanwhile, in Tenochtitlan, Montezuma listened to what his spies told him. He watched and waited.

Activities

I You read on page 42 that Cortes did a very strange thing. He burnt all the boats which brought them to Mexico.

Why do you think he did this?

2 Look at Source B. The Aztecs painted this picture. Now look at Source A. Do you think that the Aztecs painted this picture as well? Try to explain what you have decided.

3 a Can you say which man is Cortes in Source A? Why do you think this?
  b Which person is Cortes in Source B? Why do you think this?
  c Which are the Aztecs in Source B? How do you know?

This Aztec picture shows Montezuma and some nobles giving presents to Cortes. A woman called Marina is standing behind Cortes. She was very useful to him because she could speak Spanish and Nahuatl, the Aztec language.

Montezuma was worried. No one had been able to stop these strange foreigners from marching further and further into the Aztec empire. Were they from from a hostile tribe across the sea, or were they something worse? It was a special year in the Aztec calendar. The Aztec priests said the god Quetzalcoatl would come back to destroy Tenochtitlan and the Aztec people. Montezuma decided that Cortes and his men were gods. He did not dare fight them, even though they seemed to be threatening his empire. Instead he welcomed them into Tenochtitlan.

Everything seemed to be going well for Cortes. However, he wanted to make sure that his men were safe in Tenochtitlan. There were, after all, only 400 of them and there were about 300,000 Aztecs. The Spaniards were staying in an Aztec palace. Cortes asked Montezuma to come and stay with them. Montezuma, the great Aztec emperor, was really Cortes's prisoner. He did everything Cortes asked him to. Then Cortes began to complain about the ways the Aztecs worshipped. He hated their gory human sacrifices. Montezuma was very angry.

Things went from bad to worse. A Spanish commander panicked because he heard tales of plots against Cortes. He ordered his men to kill hundreds of Aztecs as they danced at a religious festival. The Aztecs fought back. A fierce and bloody battle began.

Source D

'Our Lord, you are weary. The journey has tired you, but you have arrived on earth. You have come here to sit on your throne.'

This is what Montezuma said when he met Cortes. We know this because a young man called Bernal Diaz travelled with Cortes. When Diaz was 70 years old he wrote down everything he could remember.

Source E

We admired the high towers, pyramids and other buildings, all made of stone, which rose from the water. It was all so wonderful that I do not know how to describe this first glimpse of things never heard of, seen or dreamed of before.

Bernal Diaz, who travelled with Cortes, wrote this description of Tenochtitlan many years later.

Activities

1 Why do you think that Montezuma and the Aztecs did not dare to stop Cortes from marching into their lands?

2 Look at Source C. Do you think that Marina was on Cortes' side or on Montezuma's side?

3 Read Source D. When people remember things after a long time they are not always right. Do you think that Montezuma really said this?

Cortes and his men managed to fight their way out of Tenochtitlan, over the huge causeways. About 300 of them survived. They then had to face a vast Aztec army at a place called **Otumba**. The Aztecs tried to capture the Spaniards alive for sacrifice. The Spaniards concentrated on killing the Aztec commanders so that there would be no one to give orders to the warriors. Cortes and his men won.

Other Indian tribes quickly joined sides with Cortes. They wanted to help wipe out the hated Aztecs. They marched back to Tenochtitlan and fought their way into the city. They destroyed everything as they went. The Aztecs fought fiercely to defend their city, but it was hopeless. On 13th August 1521 the last Aztecs were massacred. Montezuma was dead. Tenochtitlan was a smoking ruin. The Aztec empire was gone for ever.

◄ **A modern painting showing Cortes and his men fighting the Aztecs.**

Activity

Look very carefully at Source F.

The artist who painted this picture was not there while the battle was going on. Where do you think he got his ideas from?

Look through the book and find some sources he might have used.

Why did things happen?

1 Cortes did not have as many men as the Aztecs. As you have read, 400 soldiers came with him to Tenochtitlan. There were about 300,000 Aztecs. Yet Cortes fought and defeated them.

   Here are some ideas to explain why Cortes was able to do this:
   • Cortes wanted to be rich and famous.
   • The Aztecs believed that Cortes was a god.
   • Cortes killed the Aztec commanders so that there would be no one to give orders.

   Choose ONE of these ideas. How does this help to explain why Cortes and his men defeated the Aztecs?

2 a There are lots of reasons which can explain why Cortes defeated the Aztecs. You read some of these in Question 1. Write them down.
   b Now read this unit again and see if you can find any other reasons. Write these down.

9 What was life like in Spain?

Hernan Cortes had defeated the Aztecs. Their great city, Tenochtitlan, was in ruins. Their empire was no more. What would Cortes do now? Would he go back to Spain? Or would he try to build a new Spain in Mexico? Cortes had grown up in Spain at the time of King Ferdinand and Queen Isabella. What was it like to live in a Spanish town then?

Seville was a busy, wealthy town at the time of Ferdinand and Isabella. There were markets, shops and churches. There were houses for rich and poor people. Like most Spanish towns it had a large open square in the middle. Around the square were large houses and public buildings like the town hall. There were shops and small workshops on the roads which led from the square. A market was held in the main square. People went to the market to buy things like cloth, iron cooking pots, hens, geese, eggs, cheese, oil, wine and peaches. Unlike the Aztecs, Spanish people paid for these with money.

Nobles and rich merchants lived in houses with rooms which opened off a central courtyard. The floors were tiled. They sprinkled the tiles with water to keep the houses cool. Rich people had fine glass, silver candlesticks, carved wooden cupboards and chairs with soft cushions. Poor people lived in one roomed houses. Their floors were made of earth. They had wooden plates, pottery water jugs and a pile of rugs for a bed.

Hernan Cortes.

Activities

Look carefully at Source B which shows a market in Seville. Look back at Source A on page 28 which shows the market in Tenochtitlan.

a Make a list of all the things you can find in the two pictures which are **similar**.

b Make a list of all the things you can find which are **different**.

A modern painting of the market in Seville.

At the beginning of the 1500s nearly everyone in western Europe was a **Christian**. All these Christians were Roman Catholics. In Spain the Catholic Church was very powerful and very rich. There was only one person richer than the Archbishop of Toledo, and that was King Ferdinand. The Catholic Church owned a lot of land. Bishops and archbishops built fortresses on Church lands and organised private armies. This was to make sure the Church kept its land and buildings safe from enemies.

Some people from North Africa, called **Moors**, lived in southern Spain. Most of the Moors were Muslims. There were a lot of **Jews** living in Spain. King Ferdinand and Queen Isabella wanted everybody to be Christian. Hundreds of Jews and Moors were forced to be **baptised** as Christians, although many of them carried on with their old religions in secret.

A group of churchmen in Spain had to make sure that everyone obeyed the teaching of the Catholic Church. They were called the **Inquisition**. People were not allowed to do or say anything against the Catholic Church. Sometimes people were accused of saying something against the Church. The Inquisition questioned them in a Church court. If they were found guilty, they were punished or even killed.

Source C

This wooden carving was made in Spain in 1520 by a man called Felipe Bigarny. It shows Moors being baptised. The carving is now part of an altar in Granada cathedral.

Pedro Berruguete painted this picture in 1500.
It shows what the Inquisition did to people.

Activities

1 Find the answers to these questions! The answers are
jumbled up at the end of each question.

What religion were most people
in Western Europe at this time?   **NHISCARTIS**

Who was the only person richer
than the Archbishop of Toledo?   **NIKG DIDRFANEN**

What other religious groups
were there in Spain at the time?   **WJES AND ROOMS**

2 Why did the Inquisition kill people? Look back at unit 6.
The Aztecs also killed people. Why did they do this?

At the time of Ferdinand and Isabella children in Spain did not have to go to school. Children were taught what their parents thought they would need to know when they were grown up. The children of rich merchants and nobles were taught at home when they were young. They learned to read and write. The boys then went to schools run by the Catholic Church. They learned Latin, Greek and mathematics. Some of the schools were **choir schools**. In these schools the boys also learned to sing in church services. The girls stayed at home and learned singing, dancing, lute playing, sewing, painting and everything they would need to be a nobleman's wife.

The children of poor people learned to help their parents. They learned how to look after sheep, weave cloth, catch rabbits, plane wood, bake bread, sail ships and gut fish. These were skills they needed to have when they were grown up. The Catholic Church also ran schools for boys and girls whose parents were so poor they could not afford to look after them, or for children whose parents had died.

Source E

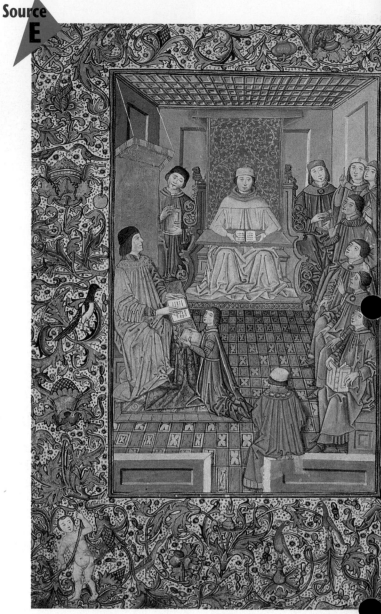

This is a page from a book made in Spain in about 1490. The picture shows a university teacher and his students. Only the sons of the very rich went to university.

This is a modern photograph of part of the front of the university of Salamanca. All the stonework was finished in 1529. At the top is a carving of the Pope who was head of the Catholic Church. Can you find King Ferdinand and Queen Isabella?

How do we know?

Look at Sources A, C, D, E and F.

1 These sources can tell us quite a lot about Spain in the early 16th century. Match up the sentences below with the right sources.

- *Spanish people were interested in learning.*
- *Spanish people were skilled stone-carvers.*
- *Spanish people were clever artists.*
- *Spanish people were skilled wood-carvers.*

2 Which of Sources A, C, D, E and F do you think **best** shows how good Spanish people were at art and craft? Try to explain why you chose this source.

3 Now look back at the pictures of Aztec art in unit 7. The Aztecs were also skilled craftworkers. Do you think that the Spanish were better at craftwork than the Aztecs?

10 What happened to the Aztecs?

Source
A

Source
B

This picture was made by Aztecs in 1520. It shows Aztecs being killed by Spanish soldiers.

All three causeways were crowded with men, women and children so thin, dirty and stinking that it was pitiful to see them. Once the city was free from them Cortes went to inspect it. We found the houses full of corpses. The city looked as if it had been ploughed up. The roots of any plants had been dug out, boiled and eaten, and they had even cooked the bark of some of the trees. There was no fresh water to be found.

Bernal Diaz travelled with Cortes. He wrote this description many years later.

As soon as the last Aztec had left Tenochtitlan, Cortes and his men moved in. The Spaniards cleared the city. Anything still standing was pulled down. Soon there was nothing left of Tenochtitlan. Cortes and his men built Christian churches out of the stones of the Aztec temples. Then they built houses and shops. Gradually the Spaniards built a new, Spanish town where Tenochtitlan had been. They called the town **Mexico City**. It is still there today.

This picture was made in the 1500s. It shows Brother Domingo, a Spanish priest, teaching some Aztecs.

The Aztecs fled from Tenochtitlan to other villages and towns. The Spaniards stopped them, and all the other Indians living in Mexico, worshipping their gods. The Spaniards stopped them making sacrifices to their gods. They built churches all over Mexico and forced the Aztecs and other Indians to become Christians. Roman Catholic **missionaries** sailed from Spain to teach them all about Jesus Christ and his mother, Mary. Most Aztecs hoped the new Christian god would be better than their old ones, who had not protected them from the Spanish invaders. Many Aztecs were not happy about having just one god. The Spanish missionaries gave the Aztecs crucifixes and statues of the Virgin Mary. Most Aztecs just added them to their household gods which they had kept secretly.

The Catholic missionaries did not only teach the Aztecs about religion. They set up church schools and taught reading, writing and Spanish. The missionaries, and most people who lived in Europe, believed that there was only one right way to live and that was the European way. They believed that there was only one god, and that was the Christian God. The missionaries thought they were helping the Indians to live good lives.

Activities

1 Look at Source A. Read Source B. Draw a picture or tell in your own words about the end of Tenochtitlan. (The end of unit 8 also tells you some of the story.)

2 Look back at Source E on page 45. Bernal Diaz thought that Tenochtitlan was wonderful! Now read Source B on page 54 again. Do you think that Diaz was sad that Tenochtitlan was in ruins?

3 The Aztecs became Christians quite quickly. Why do you think they didn't mind giving up their own gods?

Men and women came out from Spain and became farmers in Mexico. They brought horses and carts with them. The Aztecs learned how to use wheels and iron. The Aztecs and other Indians had to work for the Spanish. In return the Spanish were supposed to protect them and make sure that they became good Catholics. What actually happened was that the Spanish forced the Aztecs to work as their slaves.

King Charles I of Spain was the grandson of King Ferdinand and Queen Isabella. He did not want the Aztecs and other Indians to be treated badly. He tried to make things better, but Spain was a long way away and news and information travelled slowly. The people who went out to Mexico in the early days wanted to get rich quickly. They did not want to stay there for long. They wanted to make a fortune and get back to Spain. There they could live in luxury for the rest of their lives. They were determined to get as much work out of the Aztecs as they could.

This is part of a map of Mexico which was made by Alonso de Santa Cruz in 1550.

Thousands of Aztecs died during the fighting. Millions more died afterwards. Diseases like smallpox, measles and chicken-pox did not exist in Mexico before the Spanish arrived. When the Aztecs caught these diseases from the Spaniards, they became very ill indeed and many of them died.

Thousands of Aztecs died because of the way the Spanish settlers treated them. The Aztecs were not used to the kind of work the Spaniards expected them to do. They died from accidents, from overwork and from pneumonia.

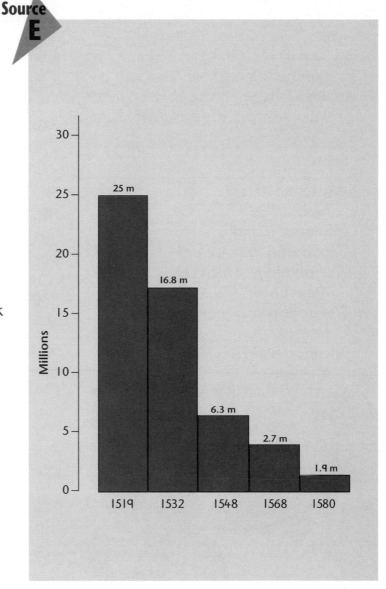

This bar-chart shows the number of Indians living in Mexico in the 1500s.

Activities

1 Look at Source D. This is a map of part of Mexico after the Spanish defeated the Aztecs. It shows men and women doing lots of different things. Make a list of all the different things you can see people doing. Do you think the people on the map are Aztec or Spanish?

2 Look at Source E.
   a How many Indians lived in Mexico before the Spanish came in 1519?
   b How many Indians lived in Mexico in 1548?
   c Why have the numbers gone down?

How did things change?

1 You have read in this unit how the Aztecs' lives changed after 1519. Some parts of the Aztecs' lives stayed the same. Others changed a lot. Read the sentences below. These are about the Aztecs' way of life.

Sentences	
Where the Aztecs lived.	
How strong and powerful they were.	
The language which they spoke.	
The gods which they believed in.	
The food which they ate.	

Copy the sentences into your book. If you think this changed after 1519, put **changed** in the right-hand column. If you think it didn't change put **stayed the same** in the right-hand column.

2 Look at what you have written in the right-hand column for Question 1. When you have put **changed**, did the Aztecs' way of life get better or worse?

3 The Spanish showed the Aztecs how to use a wheel. But they made the Aztecs work as slaves.
The Spanish taught the Aztecs to make and use iron. But they took away the Aztecs' silver and gold.

Did the Aztecs gain anything from the coming of the Spanish?

Source F

The Spanish found out where the Aztec gold and silver mines were. They found out where the Aztecs' treasure houses were. They discovered where they made their jade jewellery, their feathered shields, their rich dyes, their cotton cloth and their chocolate. The Spaniards forced the Aztecs to hand over all the precious and wonderful things they had made. Everything had to go back to Spain. They forced the Aztecs to work for them as slaves down the gold and silver mines. Ships sailed for Spain, laden with treasure.

Source G

Learning from Montezuma's account books the names of the places which sent him tributes of gold, and where the mines and chocolate and cotton-cloths were to be found, we decided to go to these places.

Bernal Diaz, who travelled with Cortes, wrote this many years later.

This modern painting shows the Spanish in control of the Aztec slaves.

11 What happened to Spain?

The treasure from Mexico was taken up the **river Guadalquivir** to Seville. Seville was the only Spanish city which was allowed to trade with overseas lands which belonged to Spain. It was a rich and exciting port. The treasure ships unloaded gold, silver, jade and pearls. These were taken by carts to the royal warehouses. The royal warehouses were full of sugar, cocoa, leather and skins as well. Oil, wine, glass and fine silks were loaded on to ships. These sailed back across the Ocean Sea. These were for the Spanish people who had decided to settle in Mexico.

After about 1525 the markets in Seville sold more things than those you saw in the picture on page 49. They sold maize, tobacco, kidney beans, pineapples, sunflowers, tomatoes, peppers, avocado pears, chocolate, potatoes and marrows. They sold turkeys. All these new vegetables, fruits and animals were brought to Spain from America.

Spanish nobles, merchants and businessmen grew very rich. They made a lot of money selling goods to overseas lands which belonged to Spain. The gold, silver and pearls pouring in to the Spanish king's treasury made him very rich as well.

This is a picture of the docks at Seville, in Spain. It was painted in the early 1500s.

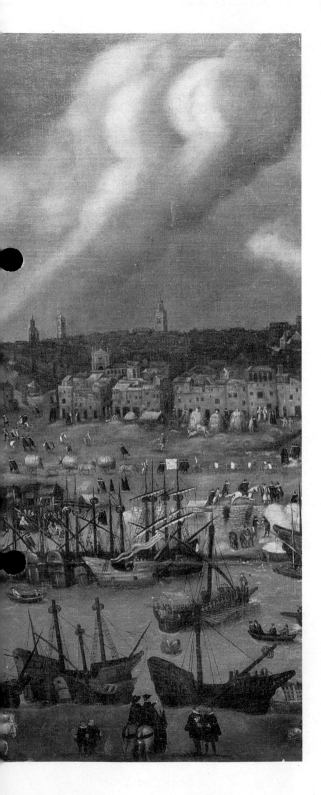

Activities

1 Spanish traders took lots of things across the sea from Mexico to Spain. They also took lots of things from Spain to Mexico.

Copy this table into your books. Then fill in the columns to say where each thing came from and where it was going to.

	Where from?	Where to?
gold		
pearls		
sugar		
cocoa		
oil		
wine		
corn		
tobacco		
pineapples		
tomatoes		
potatoes		
turkeys		

2 Why did Spain grow so rich? Here are some suggestions. Write them in your book. Which of them explain why Spain became so rich? Put a tick by the ones which you have chosen.
   • Markets in Spain sold lots of things from America.
   • The king had gold, silver and pearls from America.
   • Lots of Spanish people went to live in Mexico.
   • People in Spain liked to eat turkey more than duck.

In 1560 Spain was the richest country in Europe. Spain owned more land overseas than any other European country. The Spanish empire in America stretched for thousands of kilometres, from north of Mexico to Peru. Spanish missionaries converted millions of Indians to Christianity. Spain was the most powerful country in the world.

From his palace in Madrid King Philip made sure that his empire was run properly. He set up a special council which sent officials to Mexico and Peru who made sure his orders were obeyed. The council told King Philip what his officials were doing.

Many Spanish people went out to live in Mexico and Peru. They set up cattle ranches, vineyards and sugar and banana plantations. They built fine houses. They took plants and crops from Europe. They sowed wheat, barley and rye; they planted apple, cherry, peach and plum trees; they grew herbs like rosemary and thyme. They took African slaves to work in the sugar and banana plantations.

Other countries in Europe began exploring the American continent. By 1650 merchants from England, France, the Netherlands and Portugal were trading with people in America. 160 years earlier most people in Europe didn't even know that America existed.

Source B

This picture was made in 1594. It shows Indians working in gold mines for the Spanish mine owners.

Source C

This picture was made in 1595. It shows Indians collecting pearls for Spanish traders.

What do people say about the past?

Ilsa is telling Pedro about the Aztecs. Hank is telling Rema about the Aztecs.

'The Aztecs were lucky. They were happy with their new lives.'

— Pedro

'The Spanish taught the Aztecs to make iron. They gave them horses. They showed them how to use a wheel. The Aztecs had jobs. They worked in mines. They collected pearls.'

— Ilsa

'The Aztecs did not do well. They were unhappy in their new lives. The Spanish were cruel to them.'

— Rema

'The Aztecs became slaves. They had to speak Spanish. The Spanish destroyed Tenochtitlan. Thousands of Aztecs died from illnesses.'

— Hank

1 Read what Rema is saying. What is Pedro saying which is different?

2 Read what Hank is saying. Find some **facts**. Read what Rema is saying. Find some **points of view**.

3 What Rema is saying is different from what Pedro is saying about the Aztecs.

Do you think that this is because there are some things she doesn't know about the Aztecs?

4 Think about what you have learned about the Aztecs. Do you agree with Rema or Pedro? Why?

5 Where did Pedro get his ideas about the Aztecs from?
Where did Ilsa get her ideas from?
Where did Rema get her ideas from?
Where did Hank get his ideas from?

Now why do you think Rema and Pedro are saying different things about the Aztecs?

INDEX